# PRISMATIC DESIGN

## COLORING BOOK

45 Original Designs

by

PETER VON THENEN

Dover Publications, Inc.
New York

# Publisher's Note

Prismatic patterns and abstract shapes fill the pages of this book, making your scope as a colorist limitless. Here you are not bound by convention, as you would be if you were working with a coloring book that showed real things and everyday objects. With these abstract patterns, which do not have any built-in color associations, you can play with color with absolute freedom. It is impossible to make a "wrong" choice.

Some of these designs may seem complicated at first glance, but you will quickly discover that they are all made up of combinations of repeated shapes or parts. Color them to emphasize any aspect of the design you wish. Some elements you may want to tone down with quiet, subdued color; others you may want to make an exciting explosion of brilliant colors. Use whatever scheme you wish and the finished design will be uniquely your own. No one else—not even the original artist—will have seen it the way you have!

---

Published in Canada by General Publishing Company, Ltd., 30 Lesmill Road, Don Mills, Toronto, Ontario.
Published in the United Kingdom by Constable and Company, Ltd., 10 Orange Street, London WC2H 7EG.

**Prismatic Design Coloring Book** is a new work, first published by Dover Publications, Inc., in 1978.

DOVER *Pictorial Archive* SERIES

**Prismatic Design Coloring Book** belongs to the Dover Pictorial Archive Series. Up to four illustrations from this book may be reproduced on any one project or in any single publication, free and without special permission. Whenever possible please include a credit line indicating the title of this book, artist and publisher. Please address the publisher for permission to make more extensive use of illustrations in this book than that authorized above.
The reproduction of this book in whole is prohibited.

International Standard Book Number: 0-486-23716-8

Manufactured in the United States of America
Dover Publications. Inc.
180 Varick Street
New York. N.Y. 10014

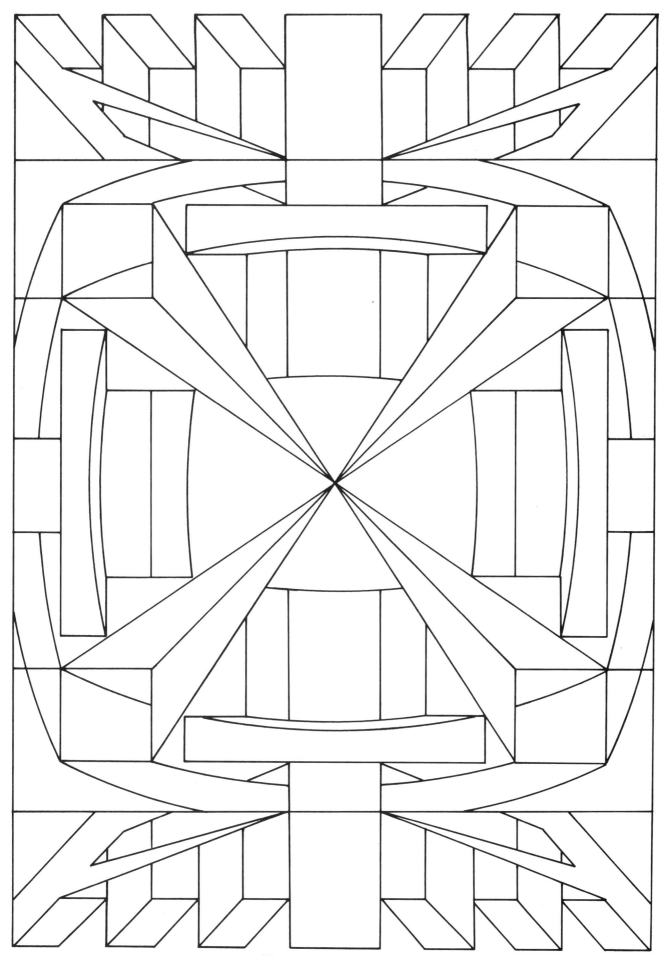

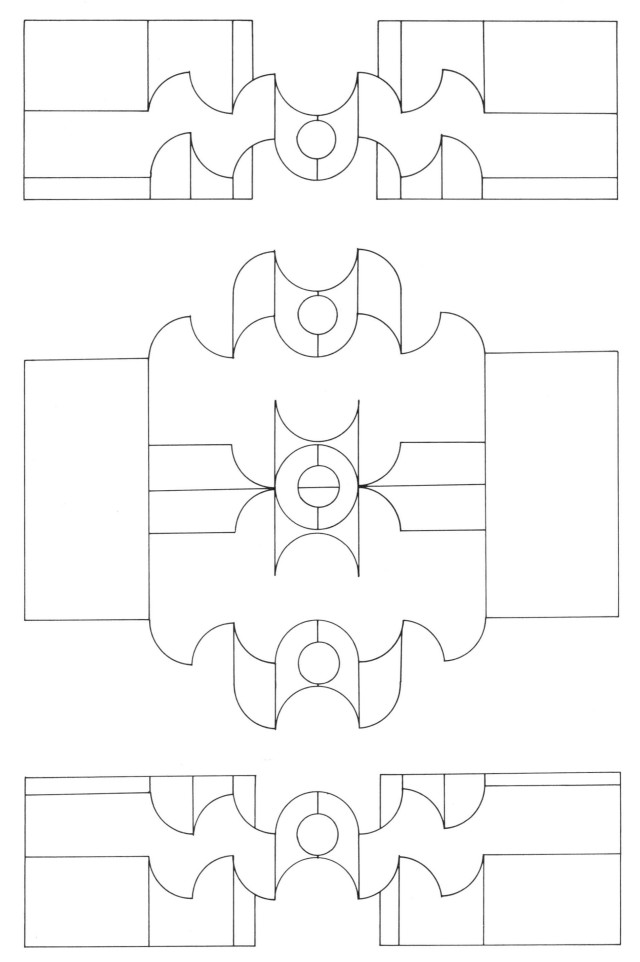

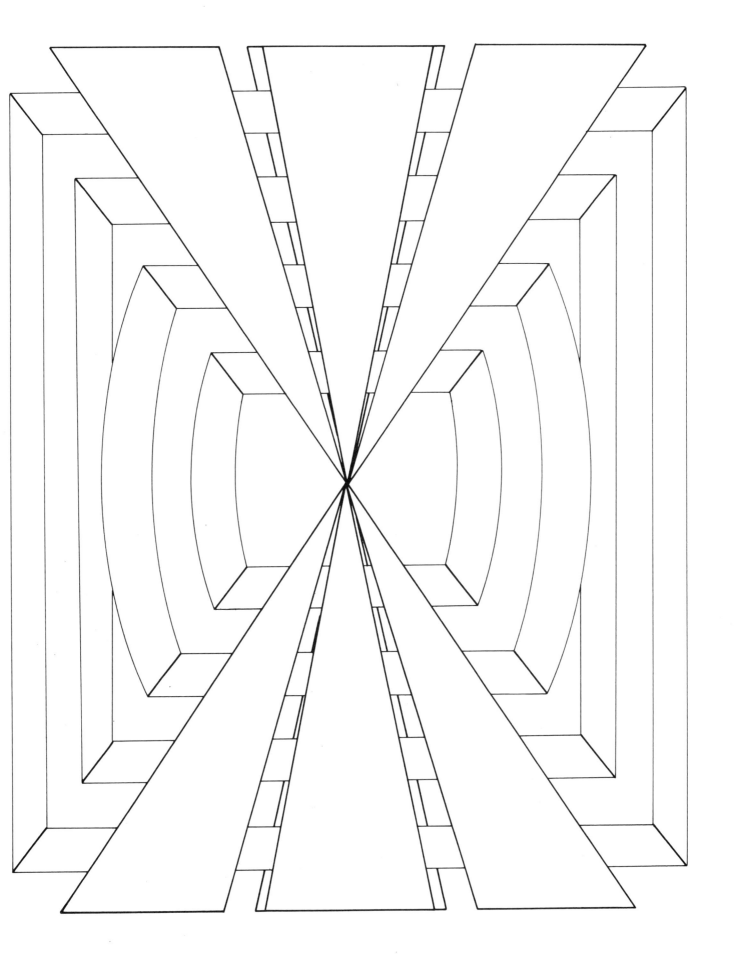

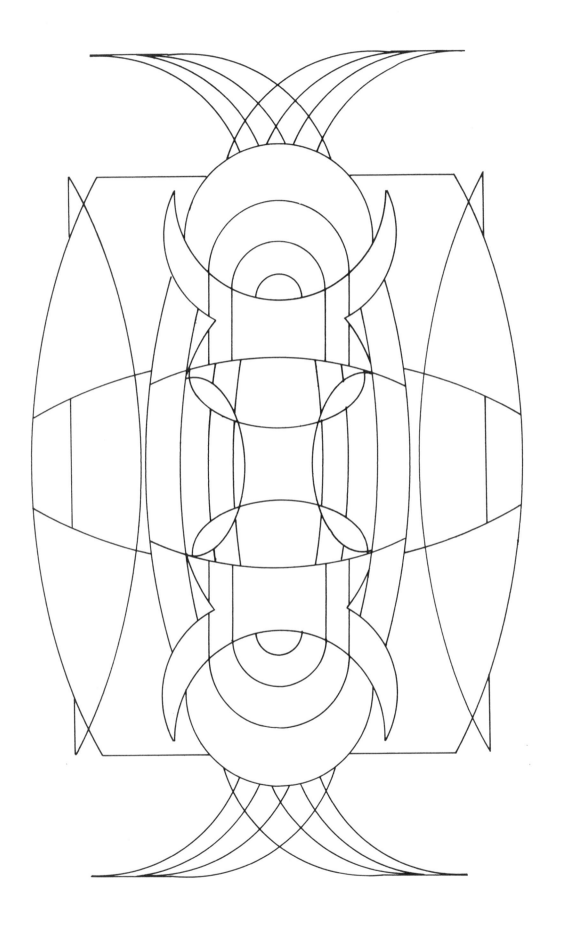

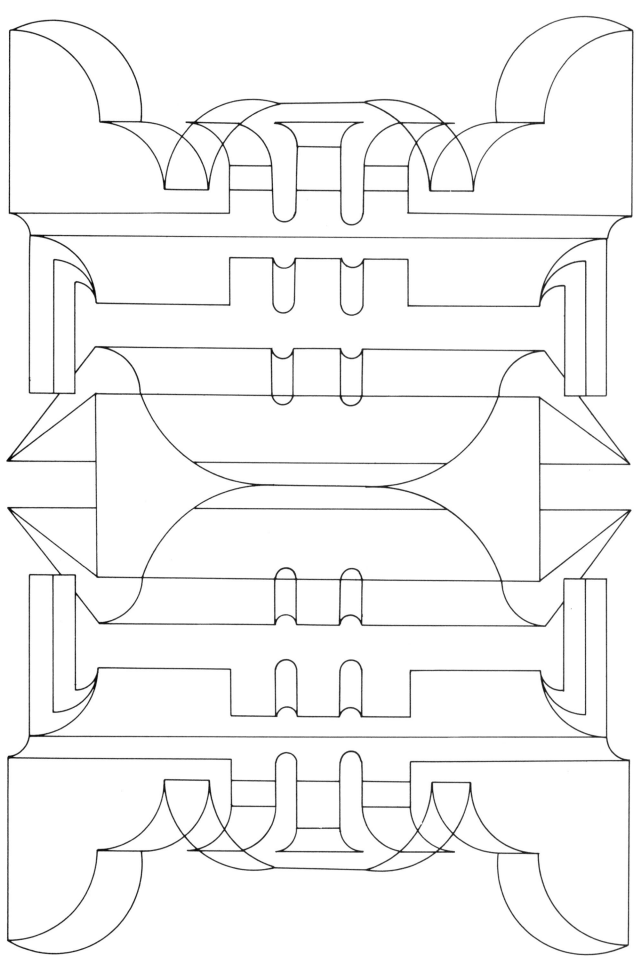

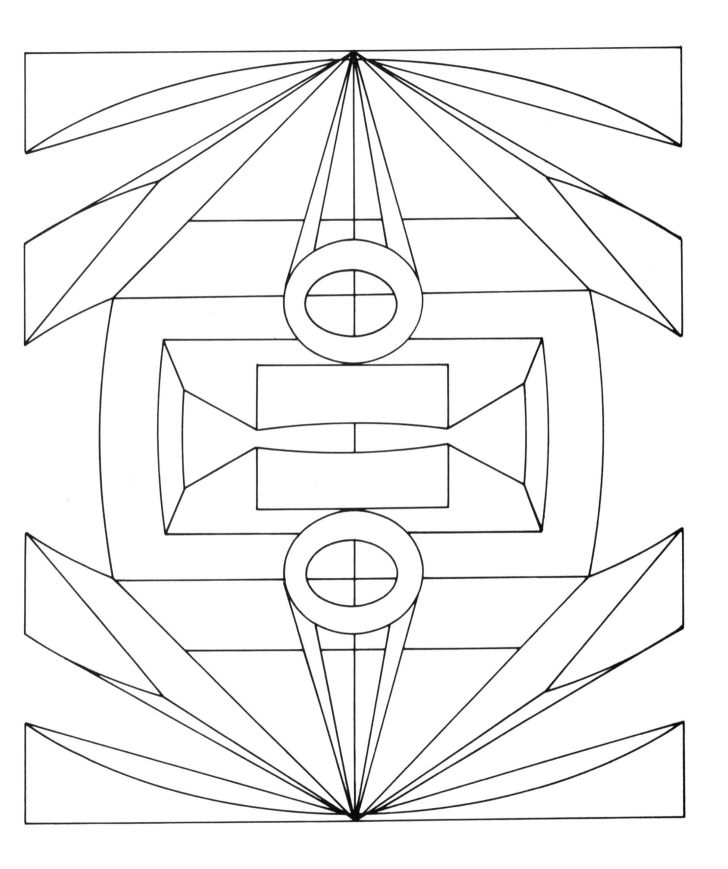

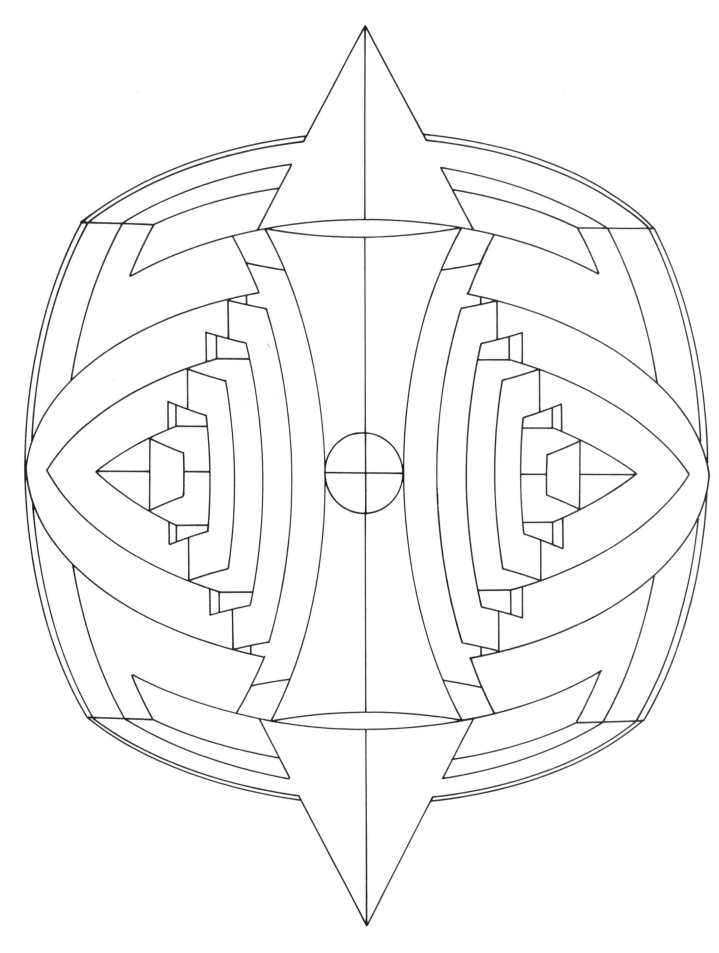

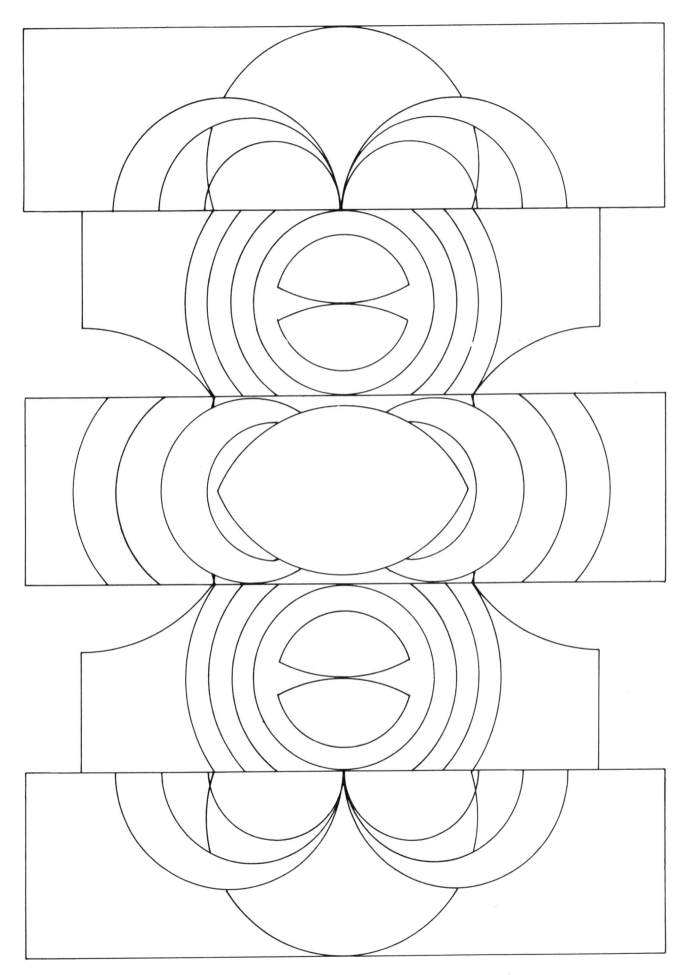

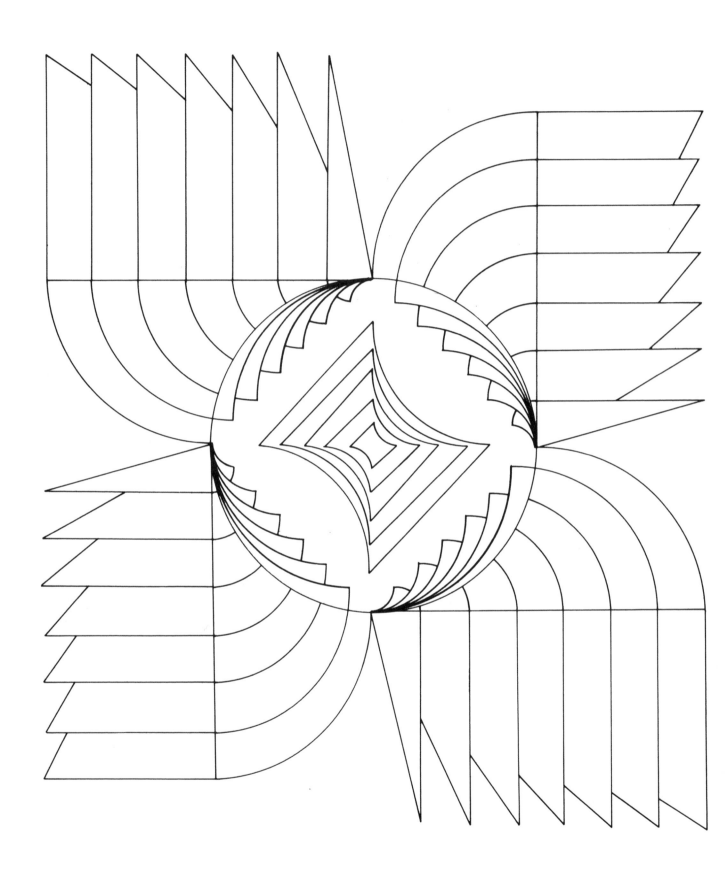

15

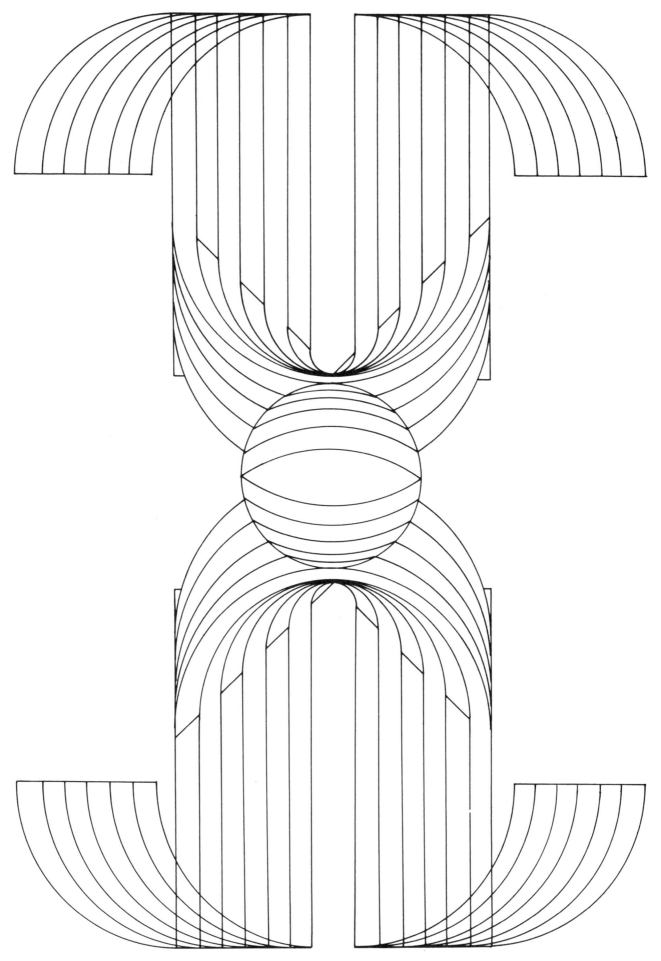

16

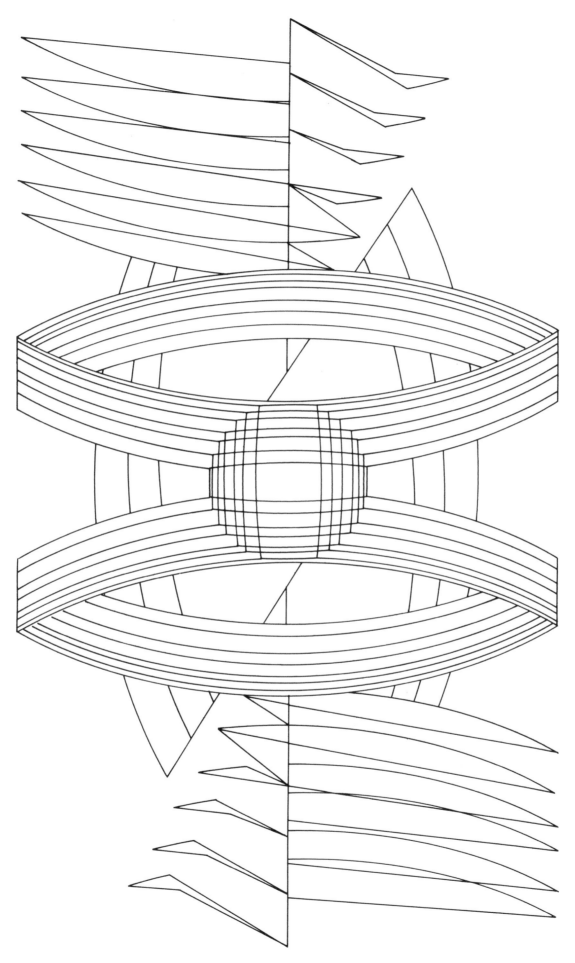

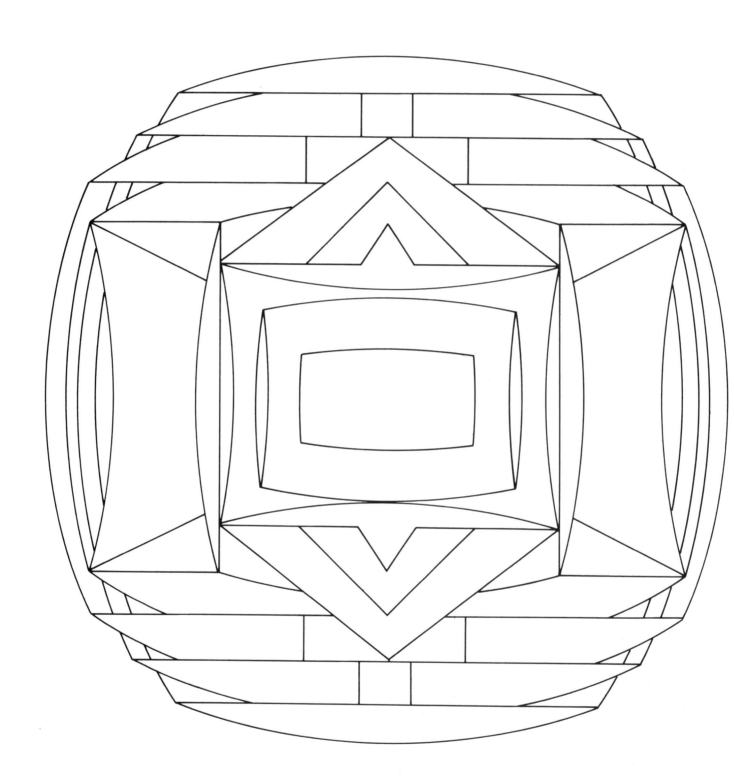

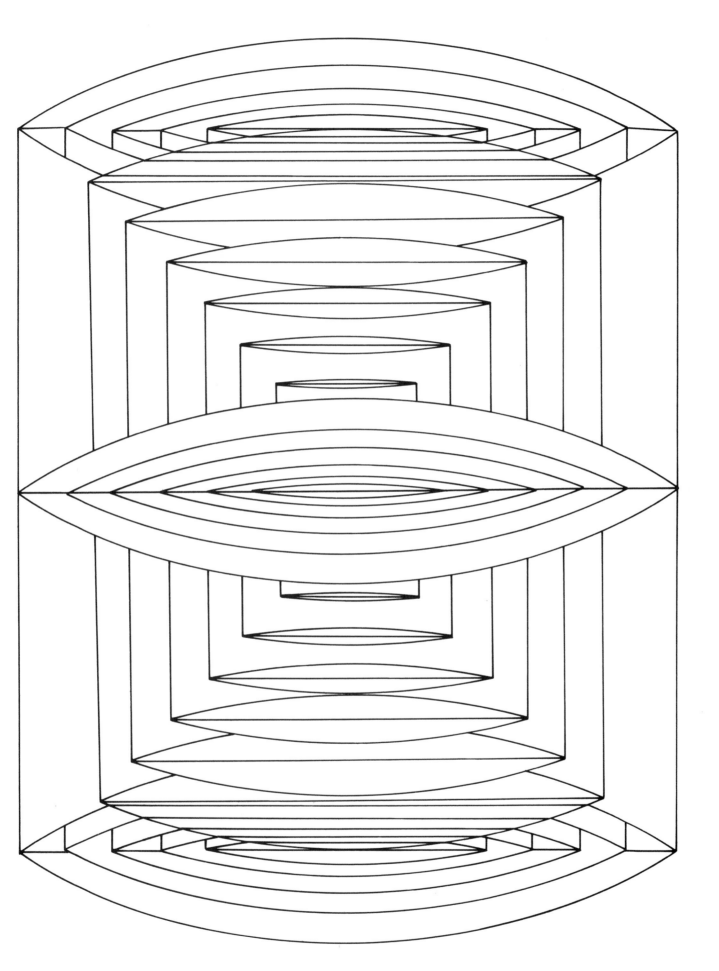

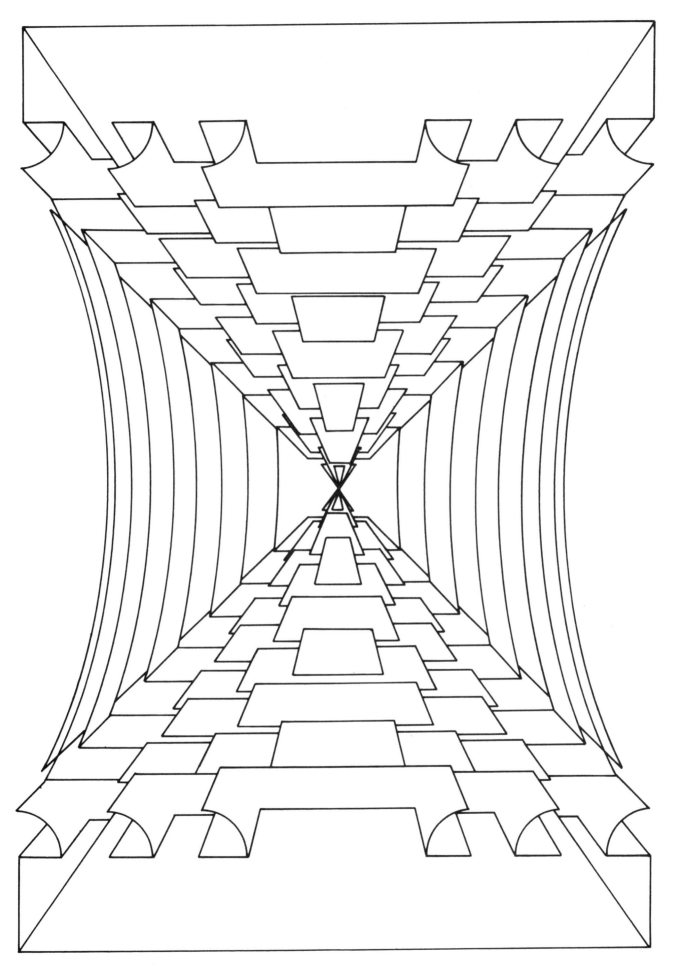

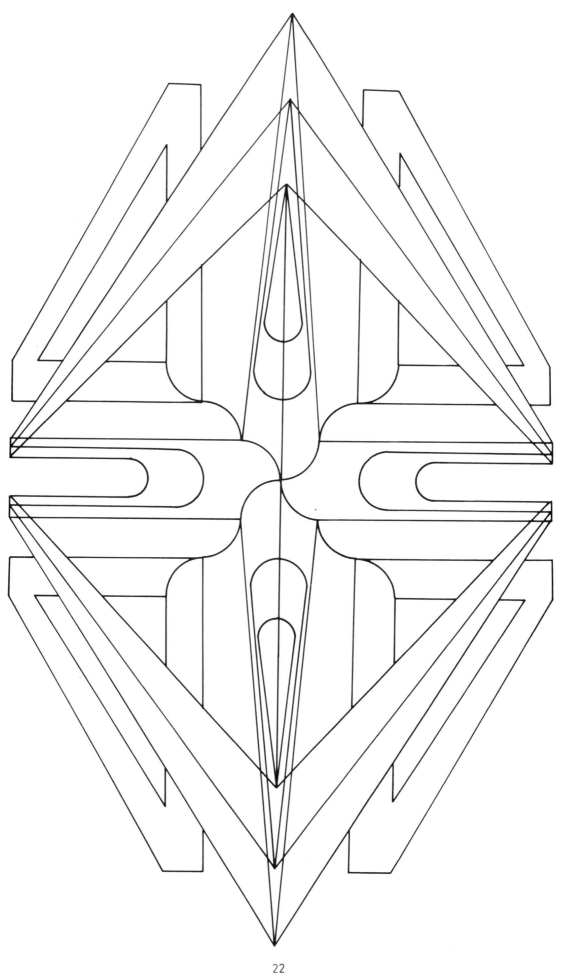

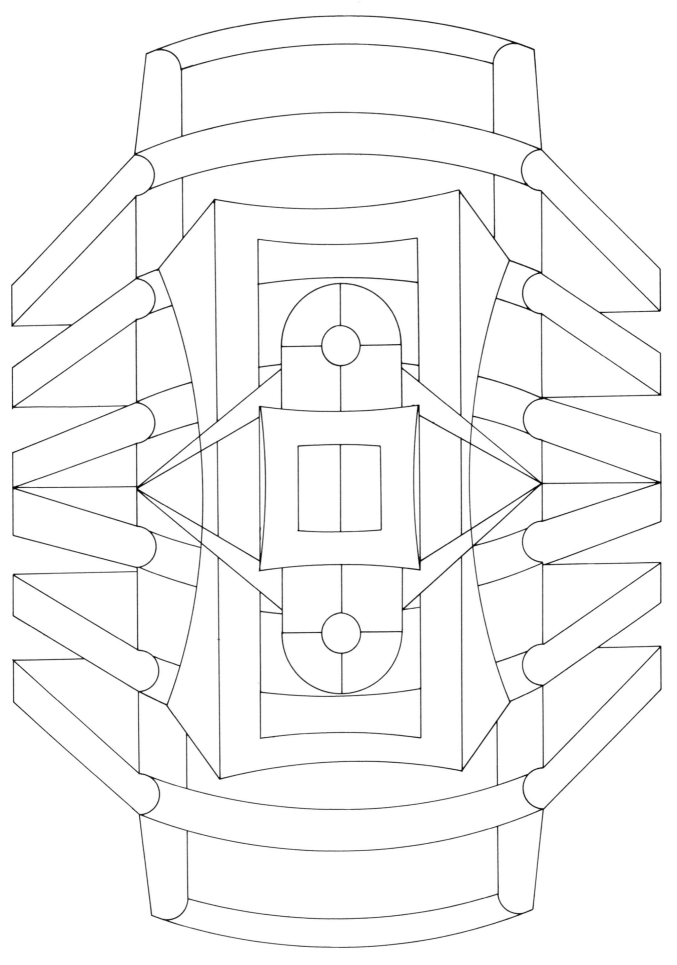

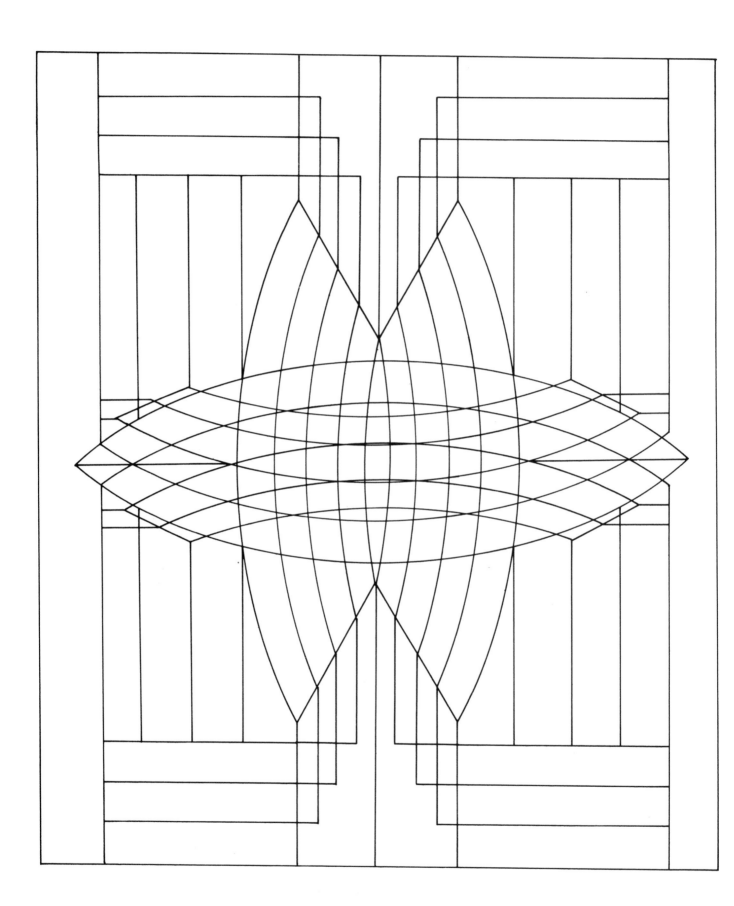

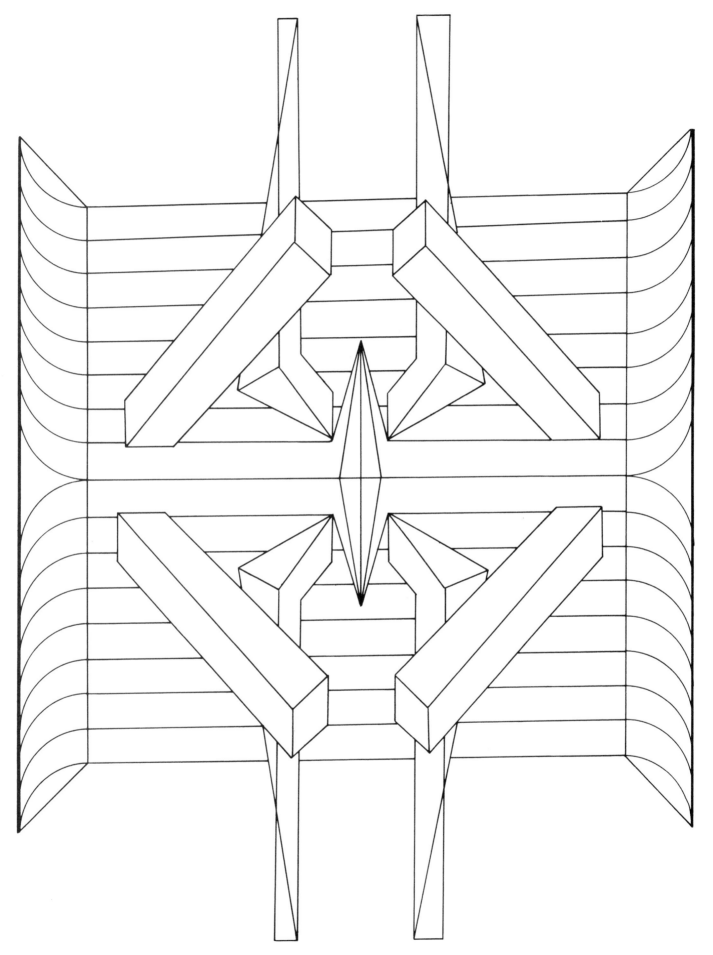

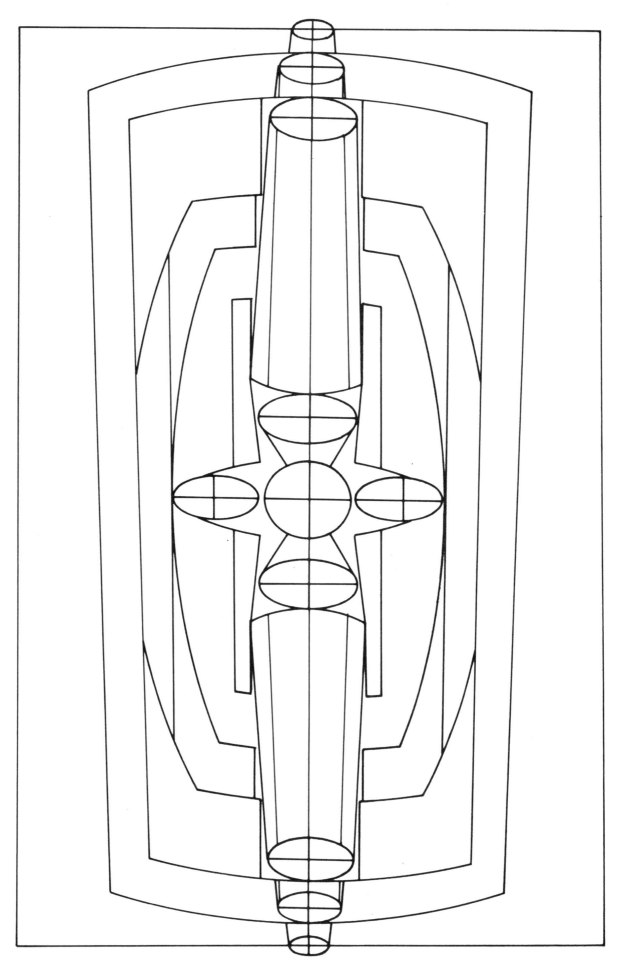

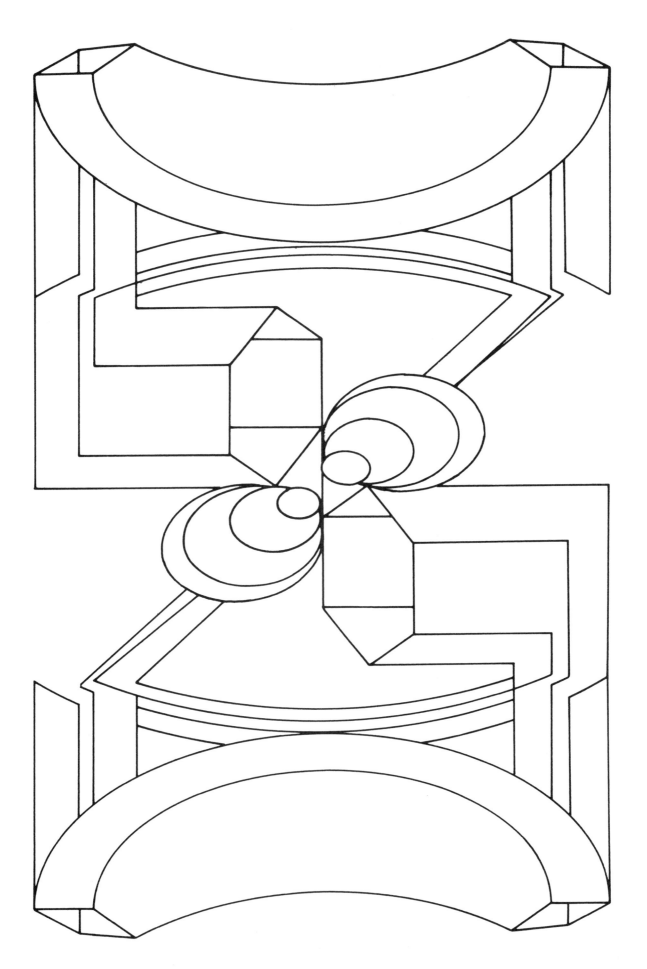

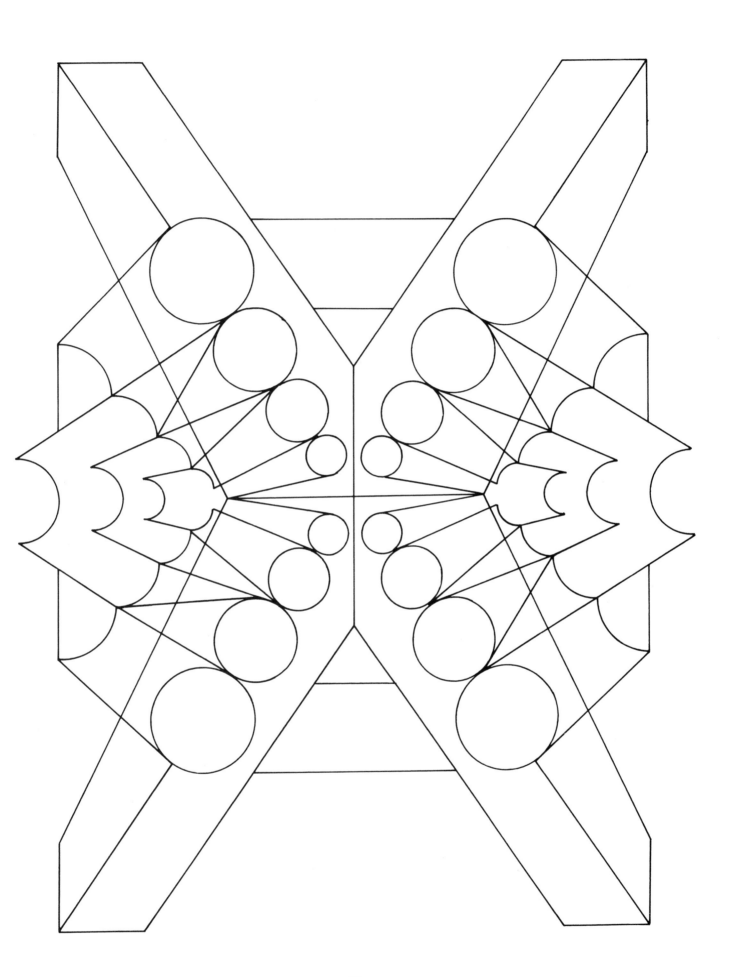

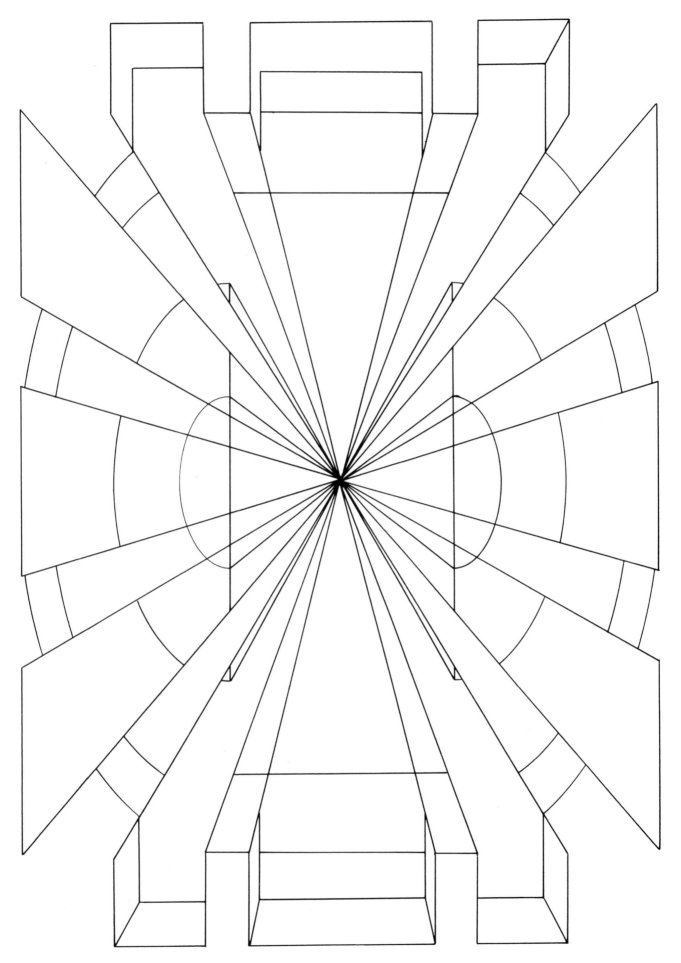

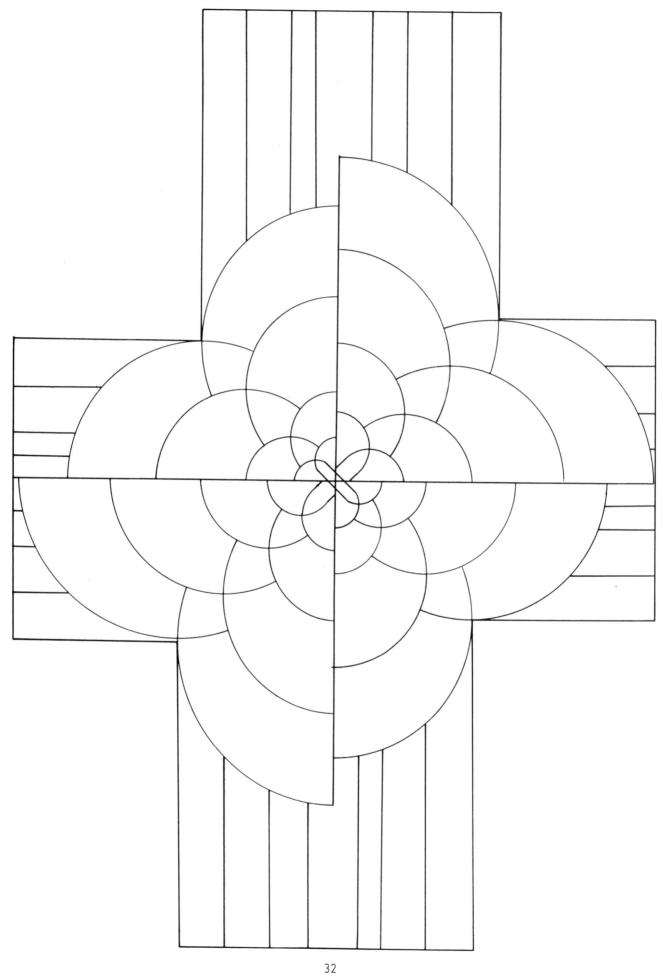

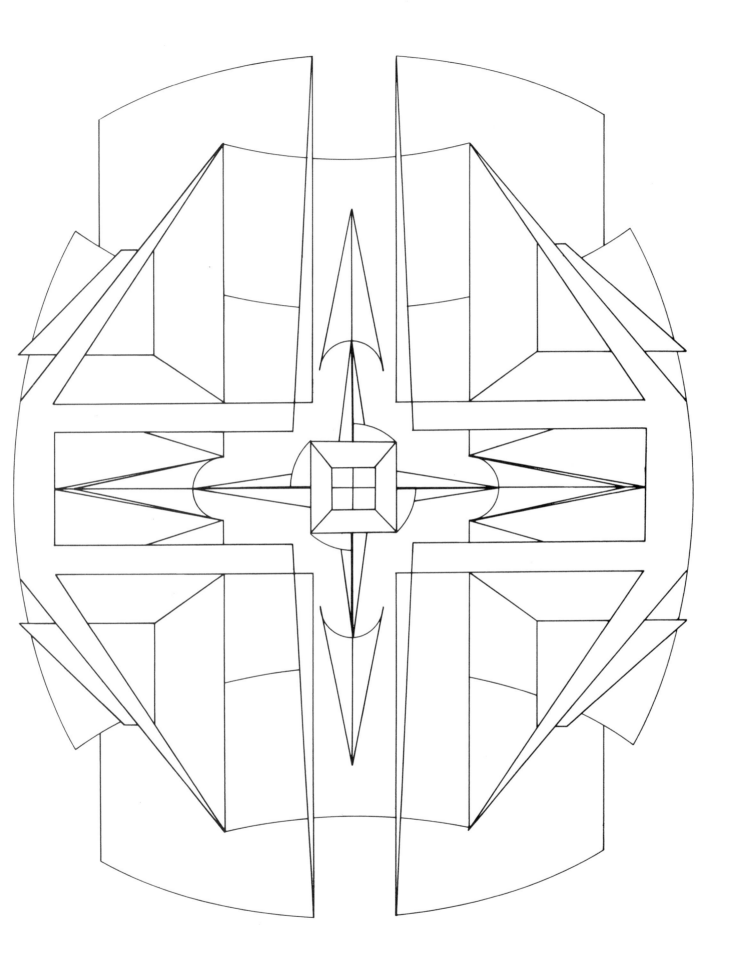

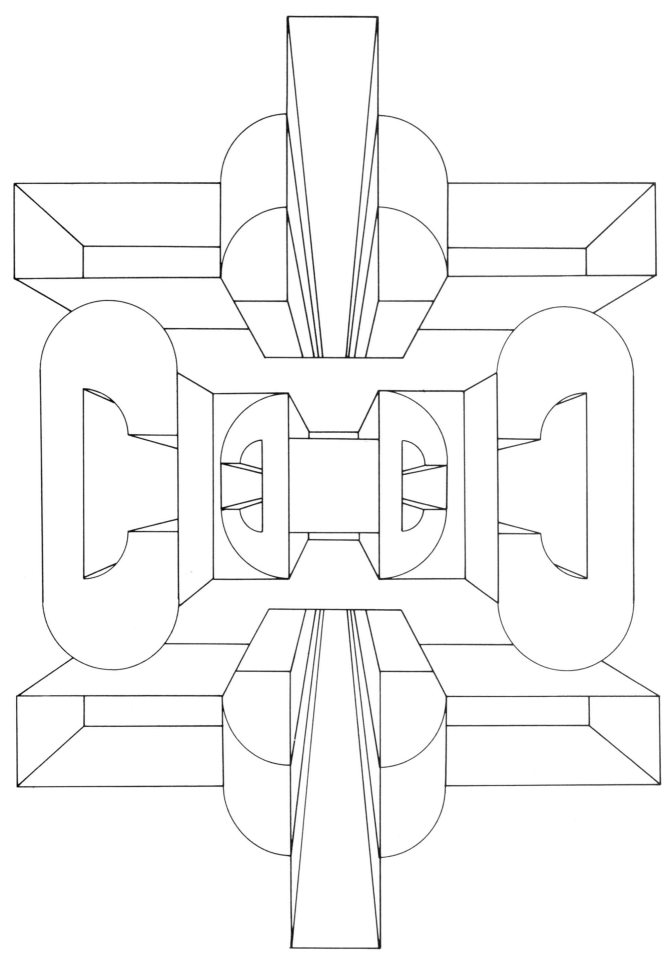

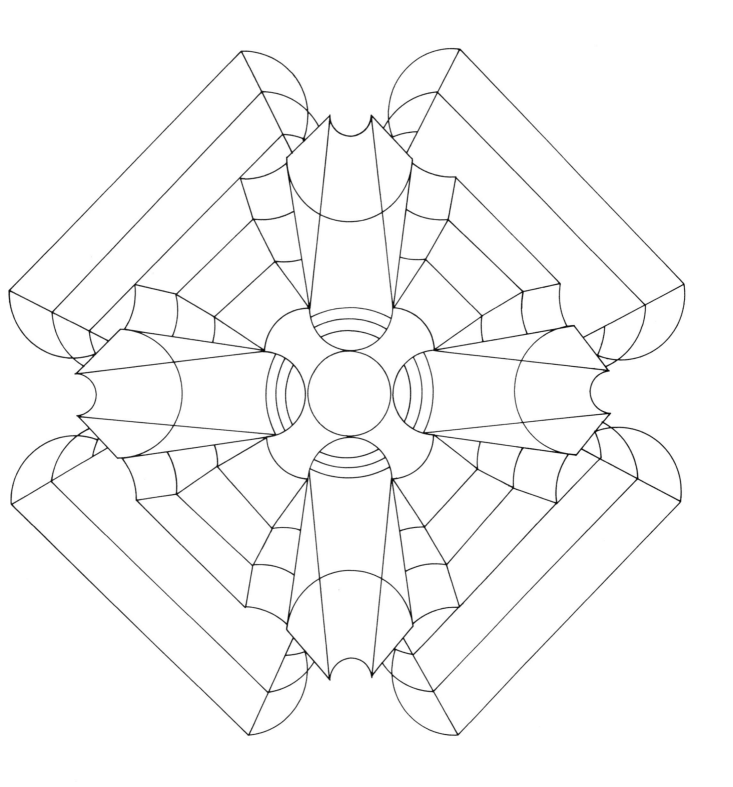

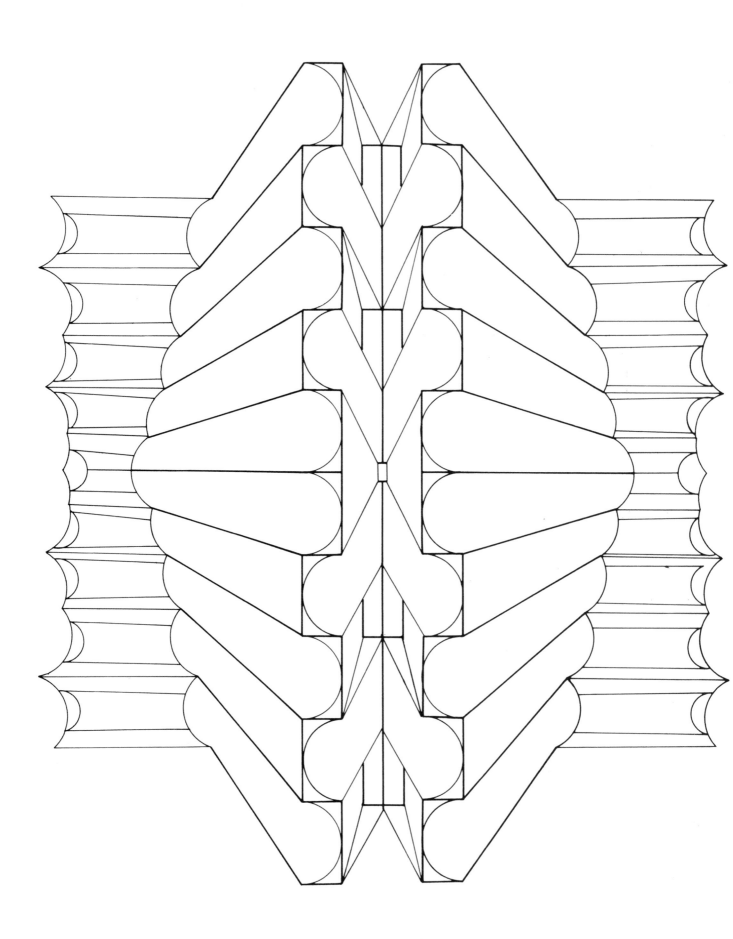

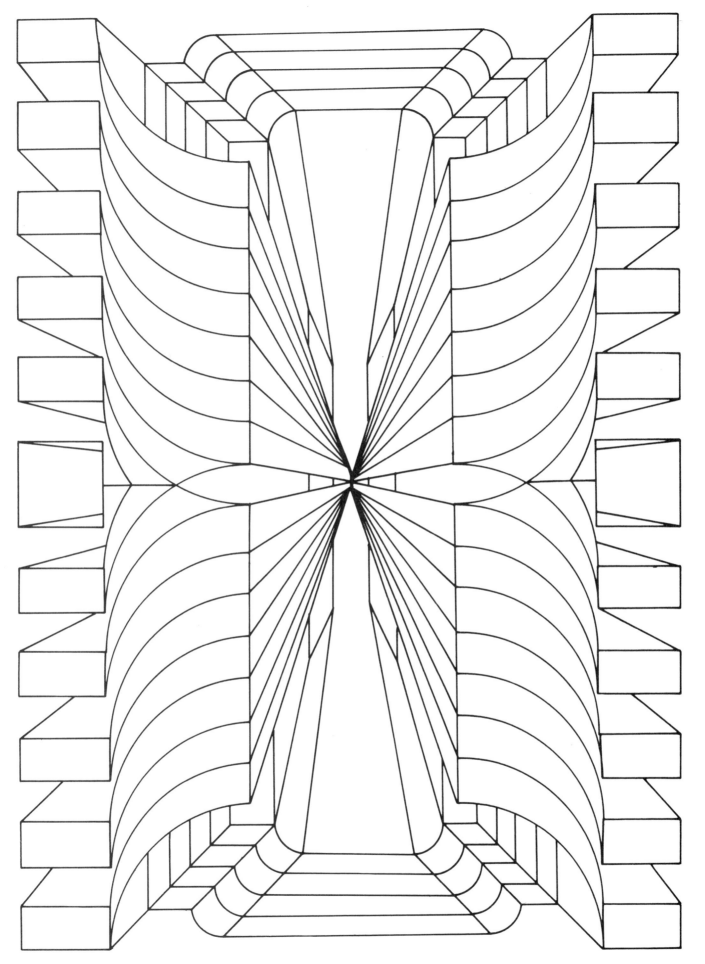

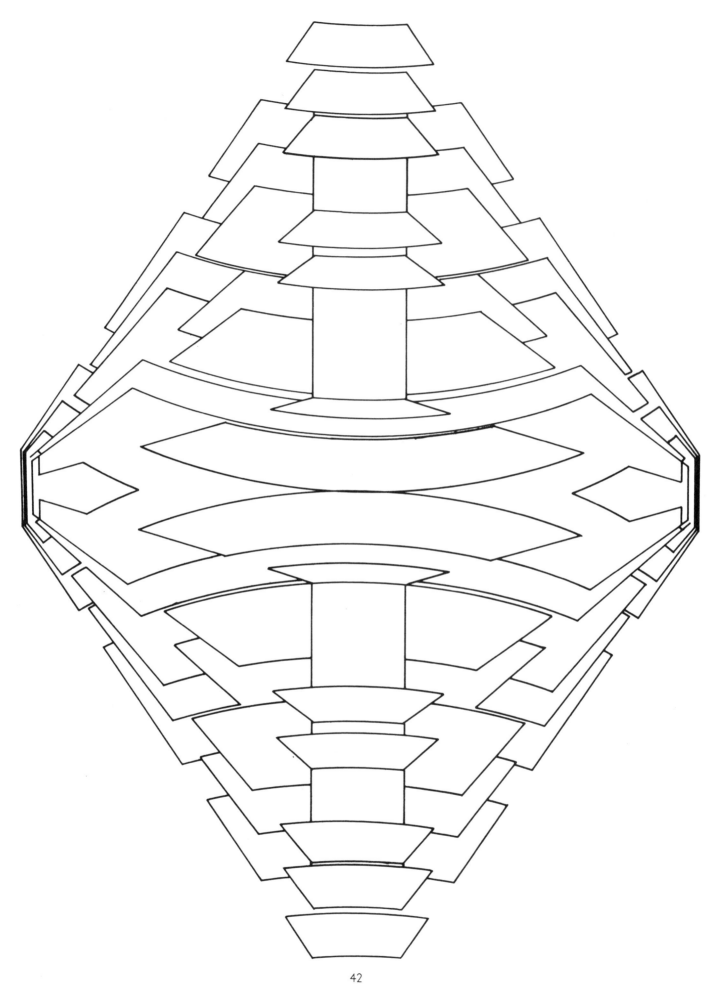

42

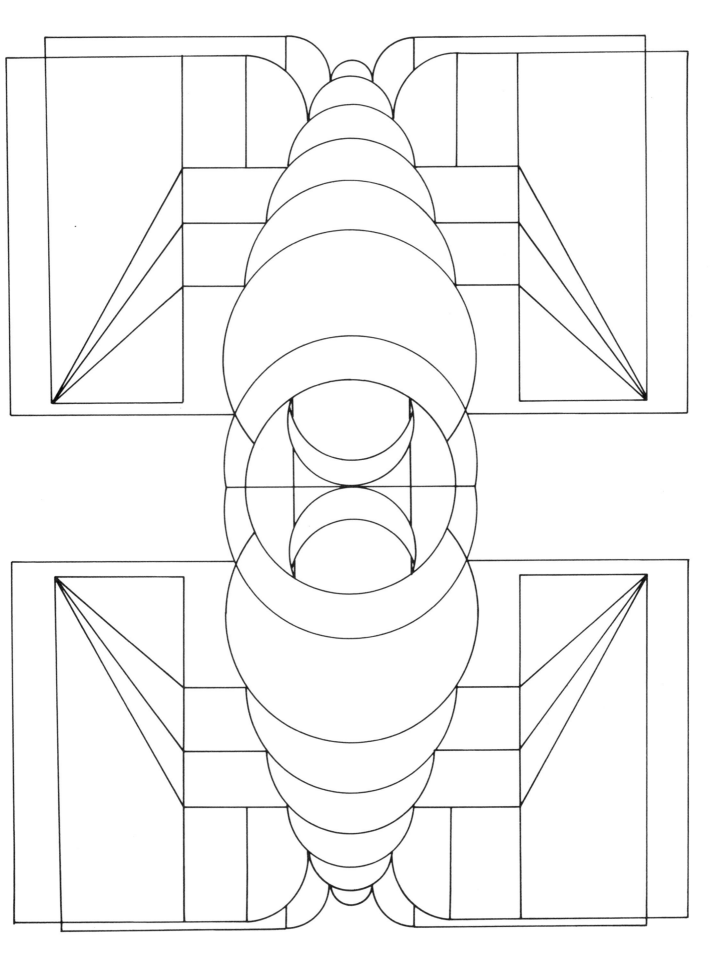

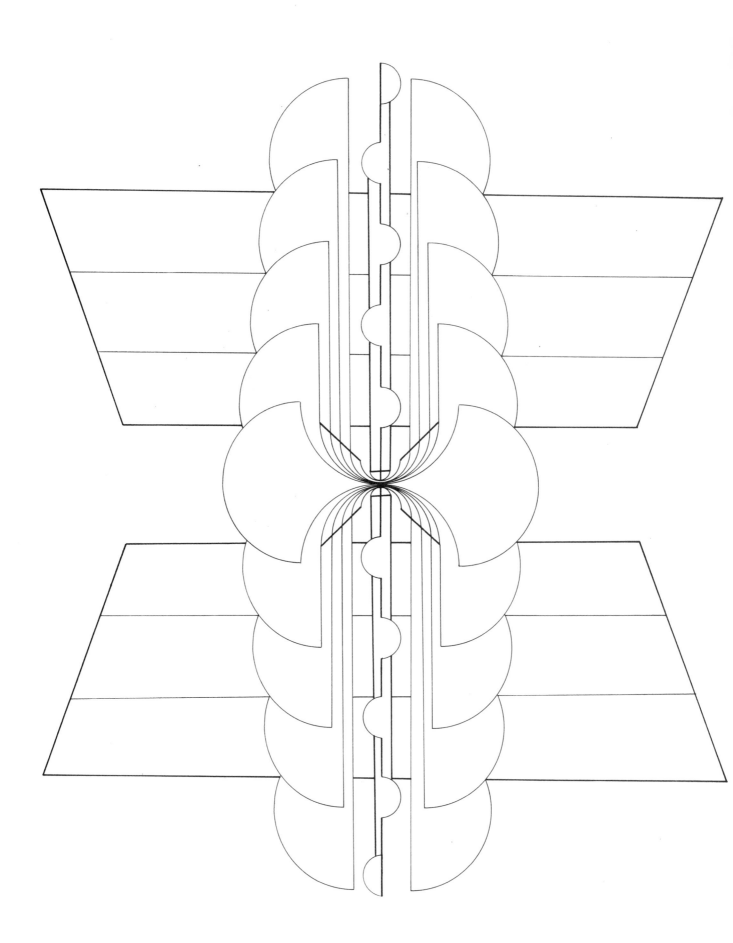

# DOVER COLORING BOOKS

Paperbound unless otherwise indicated. Prices subject to change without notice. Available at your book dealer or write for free catalogues to Dept. Coloring Books, Dover Publications, Inc., 31 East 2nd Street, Mineola, N.Y. 11501. Please indicate field of interest. Each year Dover publishes over 200 books on fine art, music, crafts and needlework, antiques, languages, literature, children's books, chess, cookery, nature, anthropology, science, mathematics, and other areas.

*Manufactured in the U.S.A.*